Whatever ou
the night sl
clear night and with
of stars, each with its own unique colour and brightness.

If we have access to a telescope we multiply greatly the number of stars we can see. The most powerful modern telescopes have revealed a Universe that is larger and more majestic than anyone could ever have imagined. Sometimes there are special sights such as an eclipse, a comet, a shooting star or a planetary alignment.

But does this beautiful Universe have a message for mankind? The first two verses of Psalm 19 summarise the message of the stars:

> The heavens declare the glory of God; And the firmament shows His handiwork. [2] Day unto day utters speech, And night unto night reveals knowledge. (Psalm 19:1-2)

These verses describe how the Sun and stars speak a message day and night to anyone who is willing to hear.

So what is the message of the stars? The main message is that the stars reveal the creative handiwork of the Creator and His glory. But the stars tell us many more things about God and the purpose of life. To find out the message of the stars we need to look to the Bible which is God's written revelation to mankind. The Bible contains many verses that explain the purpose and message of the stars.

There are people who claim to be able to interpret star signs, but we all know that their interpretations are based on guesswork and superstition. In contrast, the Bible is totally trustworthy. Psalm 19 states that the 'testimony of the Lord is sure' (Psalm 19:7), so we can be confident in what the Bible tells us about the stars.

This booklet summarises the key Bible teaching on the stars. You can see how the stars remind us of important truths about the Creator. The message of the stars gives hope in many ways - hope of forgiveness, hope of heaven and hope of knowing a glorious Creator God. I hope you find this booklet encouraging.

There
IS A
God

For since the creation of the world His invisible attributes are clearly seen, being understood by the things that are made, even His eternal power and Godhead, so that they are without excuse. (Romans 1:20)

The design of a mechanical clock reveals evidence of a designer and his attributes because of the way many intricate parts interact for a common purpose of telling the time. In the same way, the precise motions of the planets, moons, stars and galaxies reveal the existence of a Creator and His attributes.

The designer Earth orbit

The Earth's orbit has many features that are finely tuned for life. The Sun has a size and temperature that gives the Earth just the right amount of heat and light. The Earth also has a remarkably round orbital path around the Sun. Most planets go around the Sun in a highly elliptical orbit so that the distance to the Sun varies by a huge amount, resulting in large temperature variations. However the Earth has an orbit that is so close to a perfect circle that the distance to the Sun varies by less than 1.5%.

Another ideal feature of the Earth is that it rotates in an ideal 24-hour day cycle to give day and night. This 24-hour cycle is just right because if the Earth rotated faster it would experience many more storms, and if the Earth rotated slower it would heat up too much in the day and cool down too much in the night. A 24-hour day is also ideal for giving the right amount of sleep at night.

The Earth also has an angle of tilt that is very convenient for making seasons in most parts of the Earth. And the Earth has a moon that is ideal for producing tides that help life in the oceans by oxygenating the water and cleansing the coastlines.

With so many design features finely tuned to produce the Earth's orbit, it is perfectly reasonable to conclude there must be a Creator God. I have worked for the European Space Agency and designed large satellites that orbit the Earth. I know from personal experience that it takes meticulous planning and great resources to produce a stable orbit for a satellite. So when I consider the orbits of the Earth and Moon I am fully convinced that they were designed by a great Creator God.

The beauty of the stars

A building like Buckingham Palace has so many beautiful patterns and colours that it provides clear evidence of a designer. In the same way, the Universe contains so many beautiful patterns and colours that it gives compelling evidence of planning and design.

Each planet in our solar system has its own colour, terrain, gas clouds and set of moons or rings. Yet there are billions of planets in the Universe with an endless variety of beautiful designs. Likewise, stars have a great variety of sizes and colours. While some stars like those in the Pleiades constellation have a blue tinge, other stars like Betelgeuse have a red tinge. Galaxies also come in an infinite variety of shapes and colours. Even when planets die and form gas clouds they can produce stunningly beautiful sights. Gas clouds like the Orion Nebula extend for vast distances across space and contain an amazing array of patterns and colours.

Job 26:13 describes how God 'beautified the heavens', showing that God deliberately designed the heavens to be beautiful. The fact that we see beautiful colours and patterns in space is not by chance but a result of the deliberate planning and skill of the Creator.

The origin of the stars

Modern science tries to argue that the Universe could create itself through a 'Big Bang'. But many scientists will admit that the Big Bang idea is just a theory and that it does not actually explain how an ordered Universe came from nothing. The only way to disbelieve in a Creator is to say in your heart 'there is no God'. And the Bible warns that such a belief is foolish (Psalm 14:1).

Isaiah 45:18 describes how God has created the Earth for life. Modern discoveries concerning the finely tuned solar system have shown the truth of this verse. It can be tempting to go through life without thinking about our Creator. But the Bible encourages us to remember our Creator and to seek Him with all our heart (Jeremiah 29:13).

God
cares for
Mankind

> Then God said, "Let there be lights in the firmament of the heavens to divide the day from the night; and let them be for signs and seasons, and for days and years; [15] and let them be for lights in the firmament of the heavens to give light on the earth"; and it was so. (Genesis 1:14-15)

The two verses above describe how God cared for mankind by creating stars that would be a help to mankind such as providing the right amount of light for the Earth in the day and night. God even made the stars such that they would form a calendar system. God has also shown His care for mankind by creating an Earth that is supremely well designed for life.

A planet designed for mankind

The Earth has many features that are ideal for life such as abundant water and an eco-system that produces the right gases to sustain life. The Earth has an atmosphere that is just the right thickness for making a life-supporting and beautiful environment. The planet Venus has an atmosphere that is far too thick for life whilst Mars has one that is far too thin. The Earth is also unique in having oxygen in the atmosphere.

The Earth also has a water cycle that is ideal for life. Water is drawn up from the oceans by vaporisation to form clouds that are transported over the land by prevailing winds. The clouds drop water on the land which then percolates through the ground and rises up in springs. These springs supply streams and rivers with a constant local water supply for the eco-system as well as for human use.

The Earth has just the right range and abundance of materials for man to live a comfortable and pleasurable life. There are just the right types of different metals to make all the different tools and technologies needed by mankind. There is just the right range of different woods needed for constructing all kinds of artefacts including buildings, furniture, musical instruments and sporting equipment.

As a professional designer, when I look at the design of a high quality car I can see that the designer has thought of every need of the driver and passengers. When I look at the Earth I can see that God has thought of every possible need of mankind and has designed an Earth that meets all of those needs.

A celestial calendar system

The Universe provides an excellent calendar system for measuring the time of day and time of year. Of course, in modern times we use watches for timing but in past eras people often used the Sun and stars for a clock and calendar. The yearly cycle of seasons provides a clear measure of a year which is an important measure of time. The way that the moon waxes and wanes makes it possible to approximately measure monthly cycles. And the way the Sun and stars move in the sky indicates the time of day.

The Sun and stars are also important for navigation on land and sea. Even today many sailors use the Sun and stars to aid navigation. The fact that groups of stars form very recognisable patterns – called constellations – aids navigation for animals and humans.

The position of the stars

Modern discoveries have provided evidence that the stars have been designed for mankind just as the Bible says. For example, the Earth is positioned about two thirds away from the centre of the Milky Way Galaxy. This is ideal for producing a beautiful night sky that is not too bright and not too dark.

The spacing of the galaxies is also ideal for the night sky. The galaxies are not so close to the Earth that they produce too much light at night, but they are not so far away that they cannot be studied using telescopes.

The night sky is also well designed for producing occasional special effects. Comets and meteor showers are not so common as to dominate the sky but are common enough to give a regular spectacle for mankind. In addition, the moon is just the right diameter to give an occasional total eclipse of the Sun.

God's care for mankind

The Bible teaches that God has not only counted the stars but has given each one a name (Psalm 147:4). If God cares enough to give a name to each of the trillions of stars in the Universe, this shows how much he cares for His creation and especially for man who is the pinnacle of His creation.

The Bible teaches that God cares so much for us that He has numbered the hairs on our head (Luke 12:7). Some people think that they are too insignificant for God to notice them, but the Bible makes it clear that God cares deeply for individuals and knows all the details of their life.

It is incredible to think that the God of the Universe even designed the position of the stars to be a help for mankind. The psalmist said: What is man that you are mindful of him? (Psalm 8:4). God has shown great mindfulness of mankind in thinking of all his needs. The psalmist said: The Lord is good to all and His tender mercies are over all His works (Psalm 145:9). God is not a distant God but a God who cares deeply for mankind.

THE Universe IS dying

> And "You, LORD, in the beginning laid the foundation of the earth, And the heavens are the work of Your hands. [11] They will perish, but You remain; And they will all grow old like a garment." (Hebrews 1:10-11)

The Bible speaks of the aging of the stars, saying they will grow old as a garment (Hebrews 1:10-11 and Psalm 102:26). Modern discoveries have shown these Bible verses to be absolutely true – the stars are indeed fading and dying. Such Bible verses show that the Bible is the inspired Word of God.

With the use of modern telescopes it is possible to see that stars are cooling and dying. Sometimes when stars cool they explode and form gigantic gas clouds that make spectacular sights in the sky. Even our Sun is cooling and will not last forever.

Every creature and plant on Earth is subject to decay and will inevitably die. In the same way, the Universe is decaying and dying and will one day come to an end. The decay of the Universe is a reminder that something has gone badly wrong with creation. The Bible and the stars teach us about what went wrong.

The origin of death

The Bible explains that when God created the original Earth and stars there was no death and no decay. The original people – Adam and Eve – were created to live for eternity. And the stars that God originally created would also have lasted for eternity.

But the Bible also explains that Adam and Eve rebelled against God by disobeying His commands. That disobedience led to a curse on creation that involved the decay of all things including even the stars of the Universe.

It is incredible to think that the sin of Adam and Eve affected the stars of the entire Universe. The fact that the stars were affected by Adam's sin shows the seriousness of sin. But it also shows how the Universe is Earth-centred and man-centred. In other words, the Earth is not an insignificant speck in the Universe but it is right at the centre of God's purposes.

Human sinfulness

Sinning is defined as breaking any of God's commands. We have all inherited the sinful rebellious nature of Adam and so we all naturally rebel against God and His laws. The Bible teaches that all have sinned and fallen short of God's holy standards (Romans 3:21). God has commanded that we love our neighbour as ourselves by helping them and not harming them. Helping our neighbour means giving our time and resources generously. Not harming our neighbour means things such as not being angry at them, not gossiping, not stealing and not being unfaithful.

We might think that we love our neighbour adequately but if we properly understand God's standards we will realise that we constantly fall far short. Even if we are a really 'nice' character who goes out of their way to please others we still break God's laws on a daily basis. Every time we have thoughts that are lustful or angry or jealous we are breaking God's laws. We all have selfish behaviours and we all get angry with certain people.

God has also commanded that we love and serve Him with all our heart. Since God is our Creator He deserves that we spend our whole lives serving Him and doing His will. Loving God 'with all our heart' means making every decision, thought and action with the main aim of serving God and His kingdom. We might think that we love God because of our good works such as acts of charity but we never come close to putting God first in our lives as we should.

The most important way to love God is to confess our sins and trust in the Lord Jesus. Only then can we truly live a life for God and be close to God. Psalm 19 explains

that the commandments of the Lord are perfect and righteous (Psalm 19:7-8). If we look humbly and honestly into God's law we will then see we are sinners who have need of forgiveness. Psalm 19 also speaks of a Redeemer who can enable us to know forgiveness (Psalm 19:14). This Redeemer is the One who came down to Earth from Heaven to be Saviour of the world.

A
Saviour
HAS
come

Now after Jesus was born in Bethlehem of Judea in the days of Herod the king, behold, wise men from the East came to Jerusalem, [2] saying, "Where is He who has been born King of the Jews? For we have seen His star in the East and have come to worship Him." (Matthew 2:1-2)

When a baby is born, people sometimes put balloons outside the house to let others know of the birth. At the birth of Jesus, God made a very special sign by supernaturally creating a new star – called the Star of Bethlehem. This star guided the wise men to the place of Jesus' birth. Even though the star of Bethlehem came 2,000 years ago, it still reminds us today that a Saviour came and there is hope for each one of us to be saved from our sin.

A promised Saviour

The Bible explains that when the star of Bethlehem came it was recognised by the wise men from the East (Matthew 2:1).

The East probably represents a place somewhere in or near modern-day Iraq. It may be that the wise men had learnt of the Old Testament prophecy about a promised star (Numbers 24:17). However, it may be that God revealed the good news of a Saviour's birth by speaking directly to their hearts.

The fact that the Star of Bethlehem was a supernatural star shows that Jesus had come from heaven and was God manifest in the flesh. No other religion involves a supernatural sign like the Star of Bethlehem and no other religion involves God Himself coming down from heaven. These things show that Christianity is the true and only way to God. This is why Jesus said "I am the way, the truth and the life. No one come to the Father except through Me" (John 14:6).

The fact that God created a supernatural star shows that the coming of Jesus was one of the most profound interventions of God in the history of the world. The Bible explains why God sent Jesus into the world: 'For God so loved the world, that He gave His only begotten Son, that whosoever believes in Him should not perish, but have everlasting life' (John 3:16).

THE Light OF THE world

The light of the world

A star was an appropriate sign for Jesus because Jesus is the light of the world. One reason why Jesus can be described as full of light is that He is sinless and kept God's law perfectly. The Bible explains that there is no darkness in Jesus at all, meaning that He has no desire or ability to sin (1 John 1:5).

Another reason Jesus is light is because He has perfect knowledge and has revealed truth to the world through His words in the New Testament. For example, Jesus has revealed the way to heaven by explaining that we must confess our sins and put our trust in Him.

The Bible promises that if we follow Jesus we will walk in light and never walk in darkness but have the light of life (John 8:12). Believers walk in light because they have knowledge of God and understanding of His Word.

It is a wonderful thing to know God – to understand His will and commands and to pray to Him. It is a wonderful thing to walk in light. Walking in light means being able to understand biblical teaching in areas like creation, salvation and heaven. It is also encouraging to read about God's promises to help us in our daily struggles.

A risen Saviour

As John 3:16 says Jesus came so that people would hear Him and believe in Him. Jesus lived a perfect life, teaching people about the kingdom of heaven. The most important reason why Jesus came was to die on the cross. Jesus died on the cross in order to pay the penalty for our sin so that we can be forgiven.

Thankfully the Easter story does not end with the death of Jesus. The Bible records how Jesus rose on the third day and after 40 days He ascended into heaven. The resurrection shows that Jesus defeated death and this gives hope to all people.

Having faith in the Lord Jesus is not complicated. Romans 10:9 says: 'if you confess with your mouth the Lord Jesus and believe in your heart that God has raised Him from the dead, you will be saved'. However, admitting that you are a sinner who needs to repent is not an easy thing to do - it requires humility and an honest knowledge of yourself. In fact, it requires God's grace to truly repent of sin.

The King of kings

The wise men knew that they were coming to visit the most important King in the world. In fact, Jesus is the King of kings and Lord of Lords. Jesus is King because he is the Creator of all things and Lord over all. When a person becomes a Christian they do not just have Jesus as a Saviour but they also have Him as Lord, submitting to His authority and following His commands.

Even though the Star of Bethlehem is not here today we still have the bright morning star that reminds us of the Lord Jesus (Revelation 22:16). The bright morning star is the planet Venus that often appears as a bright light after dawn (and before sunset). The fact that Venus appears alone at these times as a bright light is a reminder that Jesus is a unique Saviour.

God is gracious

For as the heavens are high above the earth, So great is His mercy toward those who fear Him; [12] As far as the east is from the west, So far has He removed our transgressions from us. (Psalm 103:11-12)

When a king grants a pardon to a criminal for a serious crime and releases them from prison it is an act of great mercy because the criminal has been given the undeserved gift of freedom. When God forgives a sinner their sins and brings them into His kingdom it is an act of profound mercy because it is always undeserved and the Christian can enjoy freedom in God's kingdom. When a person receives pardon for sin and new spiritual life, the term 'grace' is often used to describe God's mercy and kindness.

Great grace

Psalm 103 gives a very powerful illustration of God's grace by comparing the distance to the stars with the greatness of His mercy towards those who fear Him and have received His forgiveness. It is helpful to think for a moment of just how high the heavens are in order to appreciate the vastness of God's mercy. The closest star to our solar system is Proxima Centuri which is about four light years away. Four light years is 40 trillion km which is a vast distance.

Another way of writing 40 trillion km is 40,000 billion km. Even one billion km is a vast distance, so 40,000 billion km is clearly an incredibly vast distance. And when you think that Proxima Centuri is the closest star and all other stars are further away, it becomes clear that the stars are an enormous distance from the Earth. That vast distance is an important illustration and reminder of the greatness of God's grace.

When we think of the nature of our sin and God's forgiveness we have to conclude that God is very gracious. In a lifetime we commit so many sins that we cannot count them or know all of them. In Psalm 19 David asked God to forgive his 'secret' sins as well as 'wilful' sins (Psalm 19:12-13). So the psalmist was sensitive to the fact that he broke more of God's law than he was aware of. This shows that he was aware of the seriousness of sin and was truly sorry for his sin.

The Bible gives examples of God's great grace in the lives of individual people. The dying thief (Luke 23) had lived an immoral life and had no time to live a morally upright life. Yet God's grace was sufficient for him to be fully saved because salvation is not based on works but the gift of faith.

Even though the dying thief is an extreme example, it is nevertheless true that every conversion involves great grace. None of us qualifies for heaven because we have all sinned against God's laws and we can never do enough good works to make up for our sin.

Grace alone

The Bible explains that we are saved by grace alone (Ephesians 2:8-9). Our faith in Jesus is a gift of God that comes through hearing God's Word. In fact it is helpful to remember that we are saved by God's Word alone, by faith alone, by grace alone, by Christ alone and for God's glory alone.

This does not mean that good works are not important. Ephesians 2:8-9 teaches that we are saved by faith for good works. So, after conversion it is important to seek to obey God's commands in order to please God and to witness to others. But we must always remember that we are not saved by good works.

At the time of Jesus, the religious leaders made the mistake of thinking that works were necessary to secure salvation. Apart from true Christianity, all of the world's religions make the same mistake of teaching some form of salvation by works.

"To whom then will you liken Me, Or to whom shall I be equal?" says the Holy One. [26] Lift up your eyes on high, And see who has created these things, Who brings out their host by number; He calls them all by name, By the greatness of His might And the strength of His power; Not one is missing. (Isaiah 40: 25-26)

When you look at ancient Roman structures like the huge Coliseum in Rome, they reveal something of the mighty power of the Romans builders. The verses above in Isaiah chapter 40 describe how the stars reveal God's almighty power. When you think that there are trillions of stars and every single one was planned and made, that helps illustrate the amazing power of God.

A powerful Creator

The Universe is awesome in size and beauty. The Universe is so vast it is impossible to fully comprehend its size. To illustrate the vastness of the Universe consider this illustration.

The speed of light is so fast that it takes just 1.3 seconds for light to travel from the Moon to the Earth, yet it would take over 30 billion years for light to travel across the Universe.

As well as being vast, the Universe also contains a staggering number of stars. The number is so vast that scientists are unable to count them. It is thought that there are hundreds of billions of galaxies and that each galaxy contains billions of stars.

The vast Universe reveals a Creator God who is powerful beyond human comprehension. When we consider that God created the stars in an instant by merely speaking them into existence, this further emphasises His supreme power. Psalm 33 teaches that we should stand in awe of God because of the way He spoke the stars into existence (Psalm 33: 8-9).

A personal helper

The power of God should encourage a respectful fear of God. But it should also encourage us because it reminds us that God is well able to help us when we have difficulties. Isaiah chapter 40 goes on to promise that God gives strength to His people. In the final verse there is a wonderful promise that God's people will 'rise up on eagles' wings and not grow weary' (Isaiah 40:31).

God's infinite knowledge is an encouragement to us because we can always trust that He knows our situation with perfect knowledge. He knows our trials and fears and He knows what is best for our life.

God
IS
glorious

O LORD, our Lord, How excellent is Your name in all the earth, Who have set Your glory above the heavens! (Psalm 8:1)

A king or queen has glory according to the greatness of their kingdom and the splendour of their crown or clothing. God is above all kings and He has a glory far beyond any glory of the world. There are several psalms that make reference to how the stars reveal God's glory such as Psalm 8:1, Psalm 19:1 and Psalm 113:4.

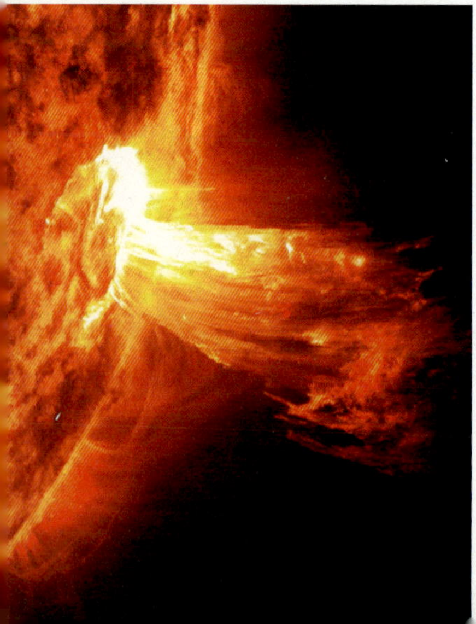

A glorious God

When the Sun is viewed close up with a special camera lens it reveals immense glory. When a powerful telescope is pointed towards the centre of the Milky Way Galaxy it reveals millions of stars that combine to produce a stunningly glorious view. When we look up at the stars we should always have thoughts of how they reveal God's glory.

Some ask the question: Why is the Universe so big if God only intended for life to be on Earth? One answer is that the Universe has to be vast in order to adequately reflect God's glory. A second reason is that God has made a huge Universe for man to enjoy exploring. A third reason is that God enjoys His own creation (Revelation 4:11).

A glorious Saviour

When Jesus came into the world, His followers recognised Him as a glorious Saviour and King. The Gospel of John describes how the people who saw Jesus 'beheld His glory'. The Lord Jesus is glorious because He is the King of kings and He is perfectly righteous.

The Lord Jesus also has glory because of His glorious victory over death when He rose from the dead on the third day after dying on the cross.

Psalm 8:5 says that God's people are crowned with honour and glory. Those who truly trust in Jesus are clothed in His righteousness and have the hope of a glorious life in heaven. One day God's people will even shine like stars in heaven (Daniel 12:3).

Plenk's Spezialführer

Nationalpark Berchtesgaden

mit

Wanderkarte, Panorama und Stadtplänen

Allgemeine Hinweise
Sehenswürdigkeiten
Wanderungen
Bergtouren
Berchtesgaden im Winter
Nachbarschaft

48. Auflage

83462 Berchtesgaden
Koch-Sternfeld-Straße 5
Postfach 2147
Tel. 08652/4474 - Fax 66277
e-mail: plenk-verlag@t-online.de
http://www.plenk-verlag.com